Silver Burdett Picture Histories

Europe's Age of Steam

Pierre Miquel
Illustrated by Claude and Denise Millet

[1983 printing]

Translated by Anthea Ridett
from La Vie privée des Hommes: Au temps des premiers chemins de fer
first published in France in 1976 by
Librairie Hachette, Paris

© Librairie Hachette, 1976. Adapted and published in the
United States by Silver Burdett Company, Morristown, N.J. 1983 Printing.

ISBN 0-382-06644-8
Library of Congress Catalog Card No. 81-86280

Contents

Europe around 1850

In 1850, millions of people wanted to change their lives, and their way of life. Never had the winds of history blown so strongly. From one end of the continent to the other, the peoples of Europe were responding to the words *liberty, expansion,* and *independence.*

The rest of the world had hardly changed. Africa slumbered and only 60 million people lived in the whole of America. Progress in Asia was far behind that of Europe—particularly of western Europe, where the population had increased by 90 million in 50 years, despite wars, poverty, and famines.

Since Europeans still didn't live very long, the population explosion was not the result of improvements in medicine and hygiene. Only one Frenchman in ten and one Englishman in seven reached the age of sixty. But everywhere the birth rate was high. From the countryside of Russia to the smokey towns of England, large families were the general rule. The English middle classes could afford to enjoy their large families, but the poor of Europe, the peasants and workers, were overburdened by their children. As one of the forerunners of socialism wrote, "The poor man's table is bare, but the bed of poverty is fertile!"

The English, Irish, Scandinavians, and Germans found themselves living in overcrowded conditions. People were leaving the countryside for the towns, lured by the prospect of work in the new industries. Although industry was growing rapidly, there was still not enough work to go around. Soon entire families were setting sail from Europe for a better, richer life in the open spaces of America and Canada. From 1846 onwards, there were mass emigrations, with tens of thousands of people embarking every year.

For those left behind, life remained precarious and uncertain from birth onwards, constantly overshadowed by threats of disease and starvation. The plague was followed by cholera, typhus, and tuberculosis, which killed people off by the thousands. Medicine and science, though making progress, had not yet discovered how to combat these terrible scourges.

The expansion of industry did nothing to improve living conditions. True, steam-powered machines were introduced into all the large textile factories and metal foundries. Railways were being built all over the industrialized countries of northwestern Europe. The first screw-driven steamships were built, made of iron. Yet in 1847 Europe suffered a great famine, during which millions of Irish, Germans, Poles, and Russians met their deaths, just as they had during the Middle Ages. What was the good of producing so many goods, if one still ended up dying of hunger?

So much poverty led inevitably to revolution. Everywhere the poor were at the boiling point, ready to rise up against the established order, to tear up paving stones, and to burn down the mansions of the rich. The French revolution of 1848 had repercussions all over Europe, including the reactionary East where the uprisings were bloodily repressed. The czar of Russia, the emperor of Austria, and the king of Prussia remained absolute monarchs. Nevertheless, Prussia and Austria were obliged to emancipate their serfs, and in 1861 Czar Alexander II of Russia abolished serfdom and liberated the *mujiks*. Liberty! Even in the icy wastes of eastern Europe, the magic word had captured people's imaginations.

In the West, too, the uprisings were suppressed and order reestablished, but the people now had tasted what independence could mean. The Italians had had enough of occupation by Austrian garrisons. The people of the German states wanted a unified country, free of the influence of bishop-princes. The Belgians, Greeks, and Poles, all victims of oppression, had already risen in revolt. In the villages of Italy, the names of Garibaldi and Mazzini, heroes in the fight for independence, were spoken with reverence. In 1824 the English nobleman and poet Lord Byron died of fever while fighting in the Greek struggle for independence. For many Europeans, a better life would be obtained by creating new, unified nations, free from the prejudices and oppression of the past, free of archdukes and archbishops.

For those western nations that had been unified for a long time and where the peasants, who lived on the land, were already free men, it was in the working-class districts of industrial towns where discontent rumbled. In Manchester, Liverpool, Paris, and the Ruhr valley, the workers demanded the right to vote and claimed that their governments had a duty to prevent them from dying of hunger. In England, trade unions were recognized; in France, the workers were given the right to vote. The first laws were passed that limited the working hours of women and children. Even though the popular movements everywhere had been harshly suppressed, the workers of industrial Europe had discovered the power of getting together to organize themselves—the power that in 1793 had been given the name of *fraternity*.

The growth of towns

	1800	1850
Frankfurt	48,000	65,000
Liverpool	82,000	397,000
Lyons	110,000	156,000
Manchester	77,000	336,000
Marseilles	111,000	195,000
Seville	100,000	113,000
Toulouse	50,000	93,000

The population in towns and country in 1850

	Total Population	Country	Towns
France	35,800,000	26,700,000	9,100,000
Great Britain	27,500,000	14,500,000	13,000,000
Russia	57,000,000	51,600,000	5,400,000

The railway network in 1850

Belgium	800 km
France	3,000 km
Germany	6,000 km
Great Britain	11,000 km
Italy	600 km

The European population explosion

	1800	1850
Belgium and the Low Countries	4,900,000	7,300,000
European Russia	35,000,000	57,000,000
France	27,300,000	35,800,000
Germany	24,000,000	35,900,000
Great Britain	16,000,000	27,500,000
Italy	18,100,000	24,000,000

But it was still not easy for the workers to form their self-help societies and cooperatives, crowded as they were in the slums of the rambling cities. As the new industries grew, the towns also grew around them, expanding in all directions with no proper planning. The crowds of young country folk who surged out of the railway stations hoping to make their fortunes in the big city found themselves homeless. In England the unemployed had no freedom at all. They were herded into workhouses, which were just like prisons, and given a bare minimum of food and shelter. The manual workers of Paris, who had arrived from the provinces of Limousin or Brittany, were housed in slums in the suburbs. The best they could do for themselves was to find a job in an anonymous workshop where the owner was never to be seen and the overseer ruled with a rod of iron. A new arrival in the city had no home, no parish, no family. He was quite alone in strange and unfriendly surroundings.

And yet Paris, London, and Hamburg held such attractions that despite being lodged in squalor and fed worse than their farm animals back home, despite their poverty-level wages, the newcomers soon settled down in these huge, bustling complexes, which seemed as if they would go on expanding forever. Activity led to activity. Wooden huts were built for new arrivals to the towns, and buildings sprang up around the railway stations. New food shops and drinking taverns were opened up everywhere. In the smart city centers, the women could gaze into the windows of expensive stores, and everyone was fascinated by the busy street life and the endless entertainment and amusement.

Crowds flocked to dances, circuses, and popular theaters, and on Sundays there was always the free spectacle of the wealthier folk walking around in their best clothes. In England the race-courses were always crowded. Money was circulating—it was no sooner earned than spent. People who had lived all their lives in the unchanging atmosphere of villages began to have the impression—or perhaps the illusion—that anything was possible for anyone. The town dwellers had the pioneering spirit.

But they were not yet in the majority. In England, where the towns were the most heavily

Imports at the port of London in 1850

In the middle of the 19th century, England was the biggest industrial power in the world, exporting all kinds of manufactured goods. At the same time, she had a shortage of raw materials, and her agriculture didn't produce enough to feed the population. A huge variety of products had to be imported—wheat from the United States and Russia; wood from Canada and the Baltic; Australian sheep; American cattle; tea from China and Ceylon; sugar, spices, and coffee from the East and West Indies; wines from France, Spain, and Portugal; fruit from the Mediterranean; cotton from the southern states of America; silver from Peru; and Californian gold.

populated of all, one person in two lived in a town. In Germany and France, there were more people still living in the country than in towns; and in central and eastern Europe, country people far outnumbered townsfolk. These country dwellers were still held back by the limitations of traditional farming methods. They could not afford to try out modern agricultural methods; there were no fertilizers and few machines, even for those peasants who had gained their freedom or were about to gain it. In the East the Russian *mujiks* and the Prussian peasants still worked like slaves, threatened by the whip on the great estates of their aristocratic masters. They were still dressed in rags and tatters, and they still lived by the rhythms of nature.

But the Industrial Revolution had made its impact on agriculture in the West, where the rich landowners had introduced machines and proved that there was money to be made from the land. Little by little, the peasants of France, Belgium, and Holland began to feel that there was some hope of a better life. There were improvements in stockbreeding, and harvests grew more abundant. They bought iron plows, mechanical harvesters, and steam-powered threshing machines. Thus the rural world was deeply affected by its contact with the new industrial civilization. The lives of French farmers were now completely different from those of the Russian *mujiks*. Technical progress had widened the gaps between nations. Anyone who traveled to eastern Europe from the West might well have thought he was journeying back in time to the Middle Ages.

In 1850 Louis Pasteur was twenty-eight; Charles Dickens had just written *David Copperfield;* and the pope had just returned to Rome, which he had fled during the uprisings of 1848. Marx and Engels had written the *Communist Manifesto,* and Wagner had composed *Lohengrin.* An entirely new Europe had been born—the Europe of steam and iron. The age of wigs, ruffles, and lace was well and truly over.

Schooling in France

In 1850, one third of French children were enrolled in a school. But that doesn't mean that they went there regularly. Between March and October, 1,000,000 of the 3,300,000 schoolchildren were absent from the classroom. They had to work in the fields with their parents.

A French worker's family budget

Shortly before 1840 a survey was conducted in Lille by Dr. Villermé. Among other things, it tells us the budget of a family working in the textile industry. If the father, mother, and one child aged ten to twelve were all working, their annual earnings would be as follows:

Father	450 francs
Mother	300 francs
Child	165 francs
	915 francs

Their expenses were as follows:

Lodging	60 francs
Food	738 francs
	798 francs

So there were only 117 francs left for clothes, housekeeping, heating, lighting, and laundry.

If one of the family wage earners fell ill or lost his or her job, it was a disaster for everyone.

Village life

In the 19th century, the peasants of the Russian steppes were 500 years behind those of northern Europe, who had been free since the end of the Middle Ages. In 1850 the Russian *mujik* was still a serf whose master flogged him and worked him up to sixteen hours a day in summer. Nine Russians in ten were oppressed villagers who earned a meager pittance working on the great estates of the nobility.

There were great estates, too, in England, in Prussia and in Austria, as well as in Spain and in southern Italy. In these countries the peasants, though freed from serfdom, were still enslaved by poverty. Many country folk were leaving the villages of northwest Europe to seek work in the towns or to emigrate to the New World. Three Frenchman in four, two Germans in three, and only one Englishman in two still lived in the country. They were often farmers or laborers who had small plots of land that they cultivated as best they could. Their crops were poor, since they couldn't afford good fertilizers or the new machines. Still, when bread was scarce, they could always fall back on potatoes. Alas, in 1847 a blight caused a terrible potato famine, and a million Irish peasants starved to death.

Even with good weather and healthy crops, the European peasant could never grow rich. Many went barefoot or wore wooden clogs; their clothes were handed down from father to son. In England their staple diet was bread, sometimes with cheese. A morsel of meat or bacon was a luxury. They drank tea, and sometimes homemade ale or cider.

Country folk helped themselves and each other as much as they could. French peasants would own a communal herd, and band together to give food and presents to an ill-nourished priest in return for his teaching their children. In winter all over Europe, peasants would gather round their firesides to listen to the old men reminiscing about the wars they'd fought in. Even in Russia, families could enjoy getting together in the warmth of a huge wood-burning stove.

8

Many Italians didn't know how to read or write, since there were very few schools in Italy. They had to pay professional letter writers to read and write their letters for them—like this young peasant woman in a village near Naples, who has had a letter from her fiancé.

A farmhouse in Brittany. Life was very hard; the peasants lived on black bread baked in the farm oven and bacon-fat soup, washed down with cider. The farm animals slept in the communal living room. In these conditions, two children in ten died before the age of two.

A steel plow called a "Brabant" after the rich, wheat-growing plains of Belgium. With its two cutting edges and two plowshares, it could plow a double furrow, its two moldboards throwing up the earth on both sides.

Shepherds in the Landes district in the southwest of France had a good view of their flocks. Perched high on stilts, they could see for miles over the flat heath, which was later planted with pine forests.

Russian peasants were still serfs, obliged to give free labor to their masters. The lord's steward could punish them for the least offence. Any *mujik* trying to avoid his duties would be flogged in public, watched by his family and neighbors.

The lords of the earth

They dominated the countryside of Europe—the great landowners like the Prussian *junkers,* the Russian *boyards* and the English landlords. They owned the land, their vast estates running into thousands, sometimes hundreds of thousands of acres. Sometimes they owned the local people, too. The land made them rich for they took more than they put into it and they exploited the peasants who did all the work.

Exporting their produce made them even richer. Ukrainian wheat and Russian taiga wood were loaded at Odessa and St. Petersburg, bound for Europe. Great boatloads of Spanish citrus fruit and Italian oil arrived at London and Amsterdam. Many landlords didn't even live on the properties that made them so rich. They relaxed in their luxurious mansions in Naples, Vienna, or Seville while others labored on their behalf.

In the West some landowners did take an interest in modernizing their farming methods, which enabled them to save labor costs and get an even better return from the soil. In England, Denmark, and Normandy, cattle, sheep, and horses were improved by better breeding methods, and increasing quantities of good quality meat were sent to the towns. They also began to study the scientific use of chemical and natural fertilizers. Research was encouraged, particularly in England and Germany where the soil was improved by marling, drainage, and the addition of fertilizers containing nitrates and phosphates.

Farming was being increasingly mechanized. Europeans imported British-made machines and the mechanical reaper invented by the American Cyrus McCormick. (Emperor Napoleon III of France even organized a race of mechanical reapers!) A Scottish-made threshing machine, powered by steam, processed grain 30 times faster than a laborer armed with a flail.

In Paris and London the great landowners controlled political life, passing laws that would benefit their interests—which meant they could grow even richer and buy even more machines. And on weekends they invited their friends to house parties in their splendid country houses.

The great English families had the finest horses in the world. They loved fox hunting and would gallop over their huge estates, their hounds in full cry, until the fox fell exhausted. Shooting was a popular English sport, too. People got together for weekend shooting parties.

English ships sailed to Russia to collect the hard timber that was needed to make strong props for mine corridors and the crossbars for railway tracks. The logs floated down the Russian rivers in summertime until they reached the seaports of the Baltic.

People were so impressed by the power of steam that they believed it could replace every kind of manual labor. This curious machine is a "steam plow." Worked by a complex system of ropes and pulleys, it was drawn across the field by a wire towline. It was expensive and

cumbersome and never came into general use. Most farmers went on using horse-drawn plows. Other machines were more efficient, however. By 1851 steam-powered threshing machines were in general use in England and France, doubling the production of wheat.

On the great plains of Belgium and northern France, sugar beet was cultivated alongside the cereal crops. Once the harvest was over, the farm laborers went to work in the local factories where the beets were converted into sugar.

In 1843 the Rothampstead Experimental Station was set up in England to encourage farmers to try out new fertilizers. These included guano, a rich manure made of bird droppings found in Peru. Laborors gathered 250,000 tons a year.

Travel by road and rail

The birth of the Railway Age began a revolution in transportation. Britain led the world in railway building. In 1829 George Stephenson's famous *Rocket* won a prize, and in 1830 the Liverpool and Manchester Railway was opened, the first line to carry passengers and freight by steam alone. It was followed by the London and Birmingham Railway in 1838. In 1842 Queen Victoria made her first train journey, from Windsor to London. All England was gripped by "railway mania"; everyone invested in the railways, including the Quakers. By 1850 the country had a national network of around 6,000 miles, as much as the rest of Europe put together.

Europe was slower to follow suit, apart from Belgium where a state system was built linking Brussels with the ports. In 1850 there were only 370 miles of track in the whole of Russia. The 404-mile track from Moscow to St. Petersburg was completed in 1851 by an American engineer, George Whistler. In southern Europe, there were only a few short tracks. By 1850 the Germans had built the Cologne-Hamburg line across the Ruhr. They had twice the length of track as the French, who thought whizzing along at 35 miles per hour was crazy! But even the French began to travel by train, and in 1850 the Calais-Paris train beat all records with an average speed of 40 miles per hour, sometimes achieving a staggering 60 miles per hour! Meanwhile, America was steaming ahead of everyone with about 30,000 miles of railroad by 1860.

Stagecoaches were fast disappearing from Britain, to many people's regret, but in Europe they were still enjoying their heyday. The "Berlin" regularly traveled the well-surfaced roads of France and Germany—on the muddy highways of Poland and Austria it often got stuck. It weighed over 7 tons, and its roof was piled high with baggage. It never went very fast—about 5 or 6 miles per hour. The landlords of staging inns prospered for travelers had to stop for food, rest, and shelter.

But nothing could stop the progress of steam. In England they even had steam coaches!

Early trains were not very safe. In 1846 there was a disaster on the Dresden-Leipzig line when the locomotive's boiler exploded! Many people were terrified of railway accidents. In fact there were more accidents on the roads, but of course they weren't so dramatic.

The tickets bought by the first railway passengers were made of copper or ivory. The French soon started printing paper ones. The first free passes were issued by the British. From 1844, third-class tickets in Britain cost a penny a mile, so nearly everyone could travel.

The Crampton locomotive was named after its inventor, the English engineer Thomas Russell Crampton. It had very large driving wheels —over seven feet in diameter, which enabled the train to reach high speeds and haul heavy loads. Because they were positioned be-

Travelers in Europe could easily get lost for the roads were not yet signposted. The driver who did not have a road map would have to stop and ask the way from a local peasant. Gradually signposts were introduced.

hind the firebox, the boiler could be placed low down, giving the locomotive greater stability. Its superb technical qualities made it very popular in Europe. The North of France Railway Company used Crampton engines for 40 years.

The first railway cars were built identically to coaches. Sometimes the body of a coach would simply be hoisted onto a truck and put back on its wheels at the other end—the first example of a road-and-rail link!

Steam power at sea

In 1850 there was about one steamship crossing the North Atlantic to ten sailing vessels. The magnificent clippers, long, slim-lined ships built in America, took only 12 days to reach Liverpool from New York, their sails swelling in the western winds, their holds crammed with cotton. Sail was to hold its own against steam for many years yet.

Steam made steady progress, however, starting with riverboats. Paddle steamers sailed regularly up and down the Rhine, the Seine, and the Thames, carrying passengers bent on business or pleasure. On the high seas, however, paddle wheels had less power than on calm rivers, and steamers found it hard to compete with sailing ships, taking from 16 to 18 days to cross the Atlantic. But in 1840 Samuel Cunard, a Novia Scotia merchant, founded the Cunard Steamship Company and set up a twice-monthly service between England and America. In 1842 the novelist Charles Dickens made the ten-day crossing in Cunard's *Britannia*—he found it rather rough!

The invention of the screw propeller gave steamships much greater power. In 1845 the *Great Britain*, designed by Isambard Kingdom Brunel, was the first screw steamer to cross from Liverpool to New York. Regular services soon started from other big ports, like Hamburg and Le Havre. The fastest ships traveled at 13 knots, burning 150 tons of coal a day. To keep them fueled, the shipping companies built large coal depots along their routes.

The busiest sea route was the North Atlantic crossing, which took thousands of emigrants to the New World to seek a better life. Then there was the Cape Route to India, China, and Australia. The British, who owned it, grew rich importing Ceylon tea, Chinese opium, and Australian gold.

In 1858 Britain proudly launched Brunel's gigantic *Great Eastern*, the biggest ship of the century; 700 feet long, she had paddle wheels *and* a screw propeller. However, she had many faults and was not a success as a passenger ship. In 1866 she was used to lay the first transatlantic telegraph cable, linking Europe and the United States.

14

There were many gaps in the French railway system. To go from Paris to Nantes on the west coast you had to get off the train at Angers and take a paddle steamer, traveling at about 12 km an hour. To go from Le Havre in the north to Marseilles in the south took 50 hours. Travelers took a train to Paris, a boat down the Seine to Troyes, another train as far as the river Soâne, and then another steamboat. Then they proceeded via the Rhône to Beaucaire where they could catch a train to Marseilles. These rail and river links existed all over Europe.

Transatlantic steamers were quite luxurious inside—for wealthy passengers, that is. This little English girl traveling with her governess to New York has a comfortable cabin on Brunel's *Great Eastern*.

Steamships were just as vulnerable at sea as clippers. After a disaster when a steamship was wrecked on an iceberg, alarm systems were devised so that passengers could assemble rapidly on deck in an emergency.

European ports had to expand to cope with the increased traffic from America. The building of the London Docks was completed with the Victoria Dock in 1855. The cranes were powered by steam.

North America had a population of 25 million, whereas Europe had 266 million. The wide open spaces of the New World attracted huge numbers of unemployed folk from England, Ireland, and Germany. Thirteen million emigrants crossed the Atlantic.

Prisoners of the mines

The Industrial Revolution created a new kind of slave—the coal miner. Coal mining had always been one of the hardest forms of labor. In the 19th century thousands of men, women, and children risked their health and their lives in the darkness underground, for miserable wages. The world had to have coal; it was needed for iron and steel manufacture, building, machine making, railways, shipping, and of course for heating houses. Britain's output rose dramatically—65 million tons in 1856 compared to 6 million in 1770.

In other parts of Europe, coal was more difficult to get at, but although they produced less, mines were busy at work in the Ruhr, in Belgium, and in the north of France. In northern France, shafts sometimes had to be sunk as deep as 1,000 meters to reach the coal seams below. The miners were carried down in tubs strung on rope pulleys. These primitive elevators were sometimes worked by a team of ponies.

Underground, the men hacked out the coal with hand picks or crowbars, and women and children dragged it back to the foot of the mine shaft, where it would be hauled up to the surface. If the tunnels were big enough, pit ponies were used to haul the coal. But most of the tunnels were too low and narrow—and anyway, it was cheaper to use women and children. Some children were employed to sit in the dark all day opening and shutting trapdoors for ventilation. Everyone worked half or totally naked because of the appalling heat.

Mine workers suffered from chest diseases and were constantly exhausted from working a 12-hour day, sometimes longer, often without a break. There were dangers from flooding, gas poisoning, collapsing tunnels, or explosions of firedamp, a gas found in the deeper mines. Thousands of laborers met their deaths, prisoners of the mines.

With no one else to help them, miners began to band together to demand better conditions. In England the Miners Association was formed in 1841. Employers had little interest in improving their lot until the government began to take a hand. In 1842 the Mines Act forbade the employment of women and of children under ten. Very slowly, things began to improve.

In the mines of the Ruhr, where shafts were sometimes sunk as deep as 500 meters, steam-driven windlasses were used to lift the ore to the surface. The coal was needed to supply the metal industries, which were steadily expanding in the Rhineland.

There was a constant danger of firedamp gas explosions. At Blanzy in France, 82 miners were killed and 45 injured in one of these disasters. In 1862, 202 miners died in an explosion at Hartley in Northumberland. Rescue workers could do little but put out the fires.

In Britain, women and children worked deep underground in the mines, half naked in the stifling heat. They worked 12 hours a day, bent double, often up to their knees in water, in the narrow tunnels which were sometimes only 18 inches high. Children of eight or nine,

In the great mines of the Ruhr, powerful steam cranes were used to take pit ponies underground strapped into special harnesses. The ponies were used to haul trucks of coal along rails. Often the poor beasts never saw the light of day again.

or even four, were sent down the narrowest seams. Women were harnessed like animals with a belt and chain to drag the trucks of coal to the mine shaft. The mortality rate, high among the men workers, was higher among children. Very slowly, reforms were introduced.

British miners breaking off from work to hold a meeting and list their grievances. Sometimes they threatened to strike if conditions were not improved. In 1841 the Miners Association was founded. This was an early form of a trade union.

The machines take over

British-made machines were putting men out of work all over Europe. Formerly workers could be proud of their physical strength or technical skill. Now factory workers lived in hardship and could take no pride in their jobs. From time to time, there were outbursts of machine breaking. But no one could halt the course of progress.

Huge blast furnaces produced more and more iron; rolling mills made the foundries ten times more productive. In 1832 James Nasmyth, a 21 year-old Englishman, invented the colossal steam hammer shown below. It could be lowered gently enough to put a cork in a bottle or used for powerful and rapid pile driving.

In the Cail factories at Grenelle, France, where one locomotive was built every day, the laborers were already working in assembly lines. It was boring work, requiring attention to detail rather than strength. In Essen in the Rhineland, the manufacturer Alfred Krupp had made his first steel cannon. In England in 1855 Henry Bessemer patented his famous "converter" which made possible the cheap mass production of steel. At Seraing, Belgium, 450 tons of coal were fed daily to two huge blast furnaces that supplied a whole range of industries.

Machines had taken over the textile industry, which employed the most workers. Britain produced about three times as much cotton as France, Germany, and Belgium put together. Lancashire became the headquarters of the cotton industry. Raw cotton arrived at Liverpool to be processed in the factories of Manchester. Both cities had already doubled in size and were the scene of riots among oppressed workers. Spinning, like weaving, had been mechanized. Factories increased production more than 5 times in 50 years.

Machines were invented to do just about everything—sewing, knitting, printing wallpapers, cutting, pounding, drilling, punching, boring. . . .

Rolling mills met the increasing demands of industry by turning metal into all kinds of shapes and pieces—plates for ships, rails for railways, tubes and pipes of all sizes. The machines consisted of powerful rollers placed close together and rotated in opposite directions by a large wheel linked by a series of gears to a hydraulic driving wheel (which was sometimes powered by steam). The hot metal was squeezed through the rollers, coming out in sheets. The workers had to use pincers to pick up the hot, flattened sheets.

In textile factories the new power looms forced the women workers to keep up an ever faster pace. Overseers made sure they didn't slack off. If they did, they would be punished or fined.

In English spinning mills women and children worked 14 hours a day! Small children were used to crawl under the looms to tie broken ends of thread. They were badly treated and often had accidents. In 1833 the employment of children under nine was banned by law.

The metal foundries of the Ruhr manufactured all the parts needed by industry. Here molten iron is being removed from the furnace in a huge bucket and poured into molds on the ground below.

The fashion of "Indian" cottons encouraged manufacturers to go in for mass production. With the invention of mechanized roller printing, powered by steam, two men could do what it had taken a hundred to do by hand. The consumer society was well on its way!

Workers in the towns

"Life for a worker simply means not dying," wrote Dr. Guépin in his report on the lives of French workers at Nantes. In northern Europe the factory towns were sprawling outwards into wretched suburbs crowded with workers who had come from the country to join the vast new industrial force.

Some people were studying the lives of these poor workers. In England they included writers like Charles Dickens and Henry Mayhew and politicians like Lord Shaftesbury. They were appalled at what they saw. Working conditions were terrible. The metal foundries were suffocating; textile factories were freezing in winter. Nowhere was there enough air, space, or light. There was no protection against dangerous machinery or chemical gases and wastes. In Lyons, textile workers were slung into harnesses so they could work the machines with their hands and feet at once! Women labored like that for fourteen hours a day.

Living conditions were no better. Mean, badly built houses were springing up. People paid high rents for a room and often shared with more than one family, sometimes in cellars underground. In Liverpool and Whitechapel, in the shanty towns of Lille and Lyons, workers slept two or three to one damp straw mattress, with no heating in winter. There was not enough water to go round, and sanitation was primitive. Diseases were rife, and children died like flies—20,000 a year in London. Meals consisted of bread and vegetable soup with occasional meat or cheese. Workers were in such poor physical condition that in France, for instance, they were ineligible for the army.

There were no laws to protect workers. Strikes were illegal and in most countries unions were forbidden. Workers who fell sick or lost their jobs were reduced to begging or to crime. In England, 2 million paupers were "succored" in parish workhouses where they were kept like prisoners. In fact, they were treated worse than criminals.

Workers had no job security. In hard times they were reduced to begging from the well-off. In Nogent-le-Rotrou, a small French town, one in seven of the population had to beg in order to eat.

Paris, 1848. A scheme was set up to assist the unemployed by giving them work and a fair wage in national workshops. But the scheme collapsed for lack of money.

At Lille in France, a squalid room with no glass in the windows rented for 80 francs a year. A well-paid worker earned only 450. Sometimes several families shared one room with no bed or blankets.

The poor found comfort in drinking barley alcohol or beer. The drinking shops in the poor quarters of Paris were always crowded. Women and sometimes young children drank there, too.

The outskirts of Berlin were no more pleasant than those of London or Lille. Working-class houses were damp and poorly heated. The workers suffered from chronic rheumatism, as well as alcoholism. Tuberculosis spread easily, and children died by the hundreds. In

Prussia, as in western Europe, the working classes were driven to desperation by poverty, and they began to adopt revolutionary ideas. On Sundays they would meet, their poverty concealed by their "Sunday best" clothes, to form illegal resistance groups.

Artisans and cottage industries

In 1850 there were still more artisans than factory workers in the cities of Europe, where they had played an important role for centuries. Many everyday items were still made by hand—clothes, hats, shoes, tools, household articles, furniture—so craftsmen were still essential. Trades like nail making and horseshoeing were still cottage industries.

Unlike factory workers, artisans lived in the center of towns, and the streets were lively with their workshops and stalls. Cobblers, hatters, tailors, and bronzesmiths worked at home or in small workshops with a master and two or more workers. The workers lived very close to their masters, and on the whole in much better conditions than the miners and factory hands. Even so, there were some whose lives were hard, like the London "slopworkers," the men and women who sewed ready-made clothes in "sweatshops." They worked up to 20 hours a day in small, dark, airless rooms, and crowded three or more to a bed at night.

Many craftsmen and women, like the silk weavers of Lyons in France and Spitalfields in London, still worked at home for large firms. Their wages fell lower and lower because of the competition from the factories. As times grew harder, these home workers experienced real poverty, and had to sell or pawn their looms to survive.

Artisans sometimes went on strike. In England trade unions had been legal since the 1820s, but employers were hostile to them and didn't take kindly to strike action. In Europe, unions were discouraged, but some artisans, including printers and bronzesmiths, formed unions in secret. In France, there were corporations or guilds that dominated whole sections of trade—like the building trade which was controlled by *compagnons,* journeymen who traveled from town to town looking for work. They belonged to the "Compagnons du Tour de France," a society which helped them get a professional training and find work and lodgings. New members were initiated into secret rites and had to complete a piece of professional work. Once admitted, they had to swear not to reveal the secrets of the trade. Thus the knowledge and skill of master carpenters and masons were passed down from generation to generation.

London chimney sweeps were often very small boys who spent their lives climbing in sooty, crooked chimneys for masters who treated them badly. But on May 1 they held a festival, dressing up in fantastic costumes and dancing in the streets to raucous music.

These strong, sturdy German peasants spent the winter months working as glassblowers at the Neustadt works in the Palatinate. They blew hard down long tubes to shape the hot, molten glass.

People were very interested in astronomy, and the Germans were making excellent telescopes. Here a Spaniard is renting his telescope so that passersby might look at the mountains of the moon.

When work was short, times were hard for small craftsmen. To get money for food they had to pawn their tools and anything else they owned. The pawnbroker returned their things when they were able to pay back the money he had lent them, plus a great deal of interest.

The silk industry in France and England had been declining for 20 years. With fewer and fewer orders, weavers had to abandon their craft. Only large companies could go on producing. Once well-paid craftsmen and proud of their skills, silk weavers began to die out.

The lower middle classes

A new section of the population was coming to the fore—the lower middle classes. These were the small shopkeepers, small businessmen, and white-collar workers. Now that they had the vote, they had a new importance. With a stable national economy, they were able to count on a regular income—about ten times less than that of the upper middle classes, but enough for a comfortable life. They saved carefully and increased their savings by modest investments in government stock or the railways, for example. Some of them put their nest eggs into buying houses, letting out rooms and apartments to local workers at high rents.

Many of them were shopkeepers—linen drapers, butchers, grocers, vintners. Butchers tended to be the wealthiest, and greengrocers and wine sellers, the least well-off. There were no big department stores as yet, but trade was flourishing. All the food stores were open to the street. Inside you could see the wife at the cash desk and the husband at the counter with an assistant or two. The money they took was immediately put aside. They believed strongly in thriftiness.

In France, England, and Switzerland "Joseph Prudhomme," or "Mr. Jones," was often caricatured by cartoonists as a portly gentleman with spectacles on his nose and an umbrella on his arm. The middle classes lived modestly and prudently, and set a high value on respectability. They liked good plain cooking, drank in moderation, and employed one overworked servant girl. They might go to the theater, but would not take their womenfolk to a music hall. On Sundays they took their families to church, and then out for a walk.

They usually had one child only. A boy would have to work hard so that he could enter a respectable profession—becoming a clerk in the civil service or the post office, for example. They would keep a strict eye on a daughter until she was ready to marry a respectable young man from the same class.

There were various rates for railway travel. In France and England, there were three classes. First-class passengers in Britain paid for padded, cushioned seats with lace doillies. Second-class passengers had wooden benches, and the third class had to stand in open cars.

The lower middle classes would travel second class. The fare from Manchester to Liverpool was only 3 shillings and 6 pence. The stagecoach would cost them 5 shillings, so the railway was a bargain. It also saved time—by train the journey was two hours less.

In France it cost money to join the National Guard, a body of private citizens trained to keep the peace. Middle-class fathers who could afford the uniform and equipment would dress up on Sundays, admired by their wives and children.

All the European currencies were stable, from the English gold sovereign to the Spanish silver *real*. In France the gold *Napoléon* and the big silver 5-franc piece remained exactly the same weight in pure metal throughout the century.

A Sunday afternoon in Amsterdam. A property-owning family would go out for a walk, dressed in their best clothes, which were smart but not luxurious. They would listen to bands playing in public parks and buy cakes for their children.

There was hardly any industry in Italy. The lower middle classes were traders or craftsmen. In Naples one of the most important trades was making fresh pasta. The spaghetti or macaroni would be cooked and hung up to dry in full view of the shoppers.

The world of the wealthy

Nineteenth-century England was the home of millionaires; there were over 20,000 of them. Eighteen had an income above £25 million. They included the bankers Baring and Rothschild. Many dukes, earls, and barons were millionaires, and their display of wealth was impressive. One thousand landowners owned a third of the country's real estate among them, and half the new apartment buildings in the cities. They had enormous households. Over a million people were employed as domestic servants in the great houses of the rich, and a total of 200,000 horses were kept for hunting.

There were fewer millionaires in Europe. France could boast only about 50. Although the French branch of the Rothschild family was doing well, they were nothing like as wealthy as their English cousins. There were practically no millionaires in Italy. But the Russian *boyards* and the great Austrian nobles had colossal fortunes and lived in sumptuous palaces.

The great lords and monied middle classes formed what was called "high society." They belonged to exclusive clubs. Many became skilled financiers or made money from property dealing. The rich were growing richer all the time. Since they held the most important government offices, they were the first to know what was happening in the world, and could invest their money to the best advantage.

The English divided their time between their magnificent country houses and London, where they spent the "Season," a round of balls and dinners. Their daughters would "come out" into society after being presented to Queen Victoria.

In summer the wealthy Europeans gathered at fashionable watering places, in winter, in Paris or London, and in autumn they hunted in the country. The ladies held literary or political salons and patronized the arts and sometimes the sciences. They led the fashion and sent their children to Catholic colleges or famous English schools. Members of high society could afford the best education.

Christian members of high society in Europe made it a duty to give to charity. This grand Spanish lady is taking her daughter to visit the poor—but she gets her servant to hand out the gifts. As yet, few people's consciences were really stirred by poverty.

Horse racing appealed to all classes of English society. At Epsom, 200,000 people would flock to see the nobility's horses running in the Derby. Betting sometimes reached astronomical figures, and the winner of the race took home up to £1 million in prize money!

One of the finest theater buildings in Europe was the Scala in Milan, where the operas of Donizetti, Rossini, and Verdi were performed. The wealthy paid large sums to sit in a box. The *prima donnas* were idolized by everyone, and ordinary people hummed popular arias.

Hunting was a popular sport among the wealthy French. They used to organize wonderful celebrations in honor of Saint Hubert, patron saint of hunters. On Saint Hubert's Day the Grand-Véfour, one of the oldest restaurants in Paris, would provide a magnificent dinner for

In England, gambling was a quick path to ruin. Fantastic sums were won or lost at the tables, and many unlucky gamblers committed suicide. Some losers were sent to debtors' prisons, like the Marshalsea, where they spent months or years hoping for better times.

dukes, princes, ministers, and rich bankers. A huge stuffed stag was set on the table to preside over the traditional carousing. Elegant gentlemen frequently passed the night away, drinking champagne and singing hunting songs.

The growth of towns

One Englishman in two, one Frenchman in four, and only one Russian in ten lived in a town. With the growth of industry and the railways, the towns of northwestern Europe were flooded by people from the country who came to seek their fortunes.

This urban growth was particularly remarkable in England. Within 50 years the population of Liverpool increased from 80,000 to 400,000; seven other cities had populations over 100,000. On the Continent the populations of Essen and Dusseldorf doubled; that of Lyons increased by 50 percent. Capital cities were the worst hit. The population of Paris grew from 500,000 to 1 million, and that of London from 1 million to 2,400,000.

Other parts of Europe were not affected in this way. Madrid and Rome remained stable, as did the cities of Russia and central Europe. In these old cities, where there was little or no industry, life remained unchanged within the ancient walls. In some cases the crumbling walls were replaced by beautiful wide boulevards, like the famous Ring-strasse encircling Vienna.

In England the old towns burst their boundaries. Red brick suburbs grew up around London. Stone was reserved for the center of the city, which was growing upwards. In Paris huge blocks of rental apartments sprang up, and property speculators had a busy time. The factory workers settled in the outskirts close to the factories of the Batignolles and Grenelle districts.

There was a total lack of hygiene in poor quarters, especially in the old parts of towns untouched by rebuilding. Lyons and Grenoble were notorious for their muddy streets. Only capital cities had paved streets, and then only in the wealthy districts. It was rare for poor areas to be lit at night. The London dockland housed 10,000 thieves and at night, people were murdered in Hyde Park. Yet the cities were lively places, crowded with all kinds of vehicles and street vendors, gay with cafés and entertainers. In Paris and London the poor at least had some free entertainment.

By 1810 coal gas was used for lighting streets. Lamplighters were employed to go through the streets each evening armed with a long pole to switch on the gas. In 1838 this system spread to Paris. Gas was used in some homes, too, for lighting and even for cooking.

The carriage that took criminals to the French law courts was called a "salad basket" (*panier à salade,* the name still used for prison vans today). With the growth of the city, the Parisian police force was not strong enough to provide proper protection for the citizens.

Large towns already had omnibuses traveling on regular routes. In Paris they were heavy horse-drawn coaches. In London, people could sit "outside" on the top deck. In 1833 a steam omnibus was tried out, but the authorities refused to licence it. There were no traffic regulations, and coachmen fought their way through with whips and oaths. All kinds of vehicles could be seen—wagons, carriages, hansom cabs, barouches, tradesmen's carts. Pedestrians needed sharp eyes and nimble feet to get across the road!

In 1840 Rowland Hill introduced the Penny Post in England. Railways took over from mail coaches, providing a cheaper, quicker service, and in 1853, red mailboxes were set up to make mailing easier.

Most town houses had no running water, and water carriers went around the streets, crying their wares. Even the poor had to pay if they wanted clean water for drinking and cooking.

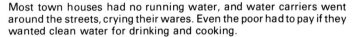

Food and drink for rich and poor

Despite all the technological progress, the people of Europe were only too familiar with hunger and all its accompanying miseries. In the worst years, like 1847, many thousands starved in Germany, England, and Ireland. Sixty-five percent of Parisians were given the free handouts of bread allocated to paupers. Malnutrition was much worse in the towns than in the country.

The wages of the workers were not enough to provide a proper diet. They lived on bread, vegetable soup, some cheese, and occasional meat. A London laborer who earned 15 shillings a week spent about 2 shillings on rent, 3½ on bread, 2½ on salt beef, and 3½ on beer and gin. In France a loaf of bread cost 50 centimes, a quarter of a worker's daily wage. A family of five would demolish the loaf in a day, washing it down with a *chopine* (½ liter) of heavily watered wine. Meat cost 1 franc a kilo and the average Frenchman ate 15 kilos a year, and he ate better than the rest of Europe. Butter was a luxury. Most people put dripping or bacon fat on their bread.

Only the privileged could enjoy really good eating. In Paris there were 200,000 of them, 1 in 5 of the population, who sometimes consumed as much as 8,000 calories a day and ate up to 12 courses at restaurants.

The middle classes were usually more sober eaters. Of course, they were in the habit of eating two main meals a day, lunch and dinner. The English middle classes didn't get out to restaurants very often, but they entertained each other lavishly at home, their mahogany tables laden with meat dishes and desserts.

In Paris both upper and lower middle classes frequented the many restaurants to be found in the districts around railway stations and markets. Some Paris restaurants, spread out over several floors, offered the same menus at different prices, depending on the quality of the cooking fat. People who ate the cheapest meals, at 1 franc, needed a strong digestion to cope with the stale dripping the food was cooked in!

Bread was still the staple diet for most people. A shortage of wheat could mean starvation, particularly in the towns that depended on the surrounding country districts for supplies. In central and eastern Europe transportation was expensive and in short supply, so it could take a long time for provisions to arrive. Sometimes when there was a food shortage, the big producers stockpiled their grain so they could sell it at a higher price. In the summer of 1847, the bakeries of Berlin were stormed and looted by hungry workers.

In Paris there was a "Big Belly Club." Its twelve members would arrive at their meeting place at six on a Saturday evening to devour mountains of food. They wouldn't leave until midday on Sunday.

Oysters were a rare delicacy, even in the luxury restaurants. But at the Channel ports they could be bought quite cheaply and eaten on the spot. The English adored oysters.

There was no way of making ice, so in winter people would cut it from frozen ponds and lakes. It was stored in brick icehouses underground, where it could be kept until it was wanted in the summer.

Health and hygiene

Thanks to advances in medicine, illness didn't always have to end in death. Doctors now used the stethoscope, invented in 1819 by R.T. Laennec, and serious studies had been made of diphtheria and tuberculosis. Claude Bernard had just discovered the function of the liver. Pharmacists sold quinine for fever and codeine for coughs. Surgery took a stride forward with the discovery of anesthetics. The first major operation under ether was performed in Massachusetts in 1846, and in 1847 a Scots surgeon, James Simpson, operated for the first time using chloroform.

But medicine was still powerless against serious diseases. Malaria raged in southern Europe, and typhus killed 20,000 Belgians in 1847. Cholera carried off 100,000 French and some 600,000 Russians; there were major outbreaks in England in 1832, 1849, and 1852. The hospitals were not equipped to deal with large numbers and were uncomfortable and unhygienic. In an epidemic, doctors prescribed chlorine, bismuth and Turkish baths. The prefect of Paris ordered rubbish carts to clean the streets. No one yet knew about germs and viruses or that typhus is spread by fleas and the plague by rats. Scientists had, however, learned that cholera is carried by water; and the rivers which supplied large cities were filthy. In 1855 London's first medical officer of health, Sir John Simon, started to create a clean water and main drainage system.

European cities were rife with alcoholism, smallpox, and tuberculosis. The poor, ill-fed and with no sanitation, were the first to fall sick and they died in thousands. In the better quarters of Paris, the death rate was 15 percent; in working class areas it was 38 percent. Few people, anywhere, lived beyond 60. Only the wealthy enjoyed cleanliness, warmth, and good food. Even among them tuberculosis, known as consumption, was common. Some famous people died of it, including the Polish composer Chopin, the English writers Anne and Emily Brontë, and the French poet Alfred de Musset.

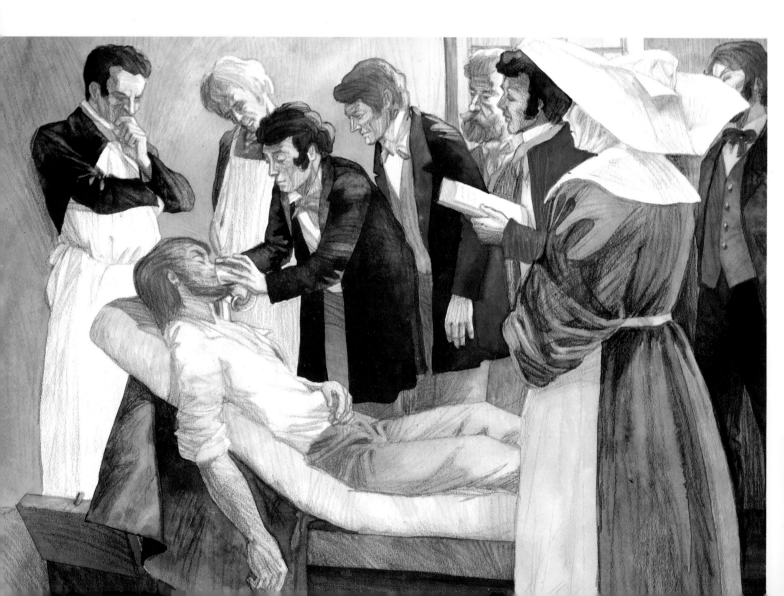

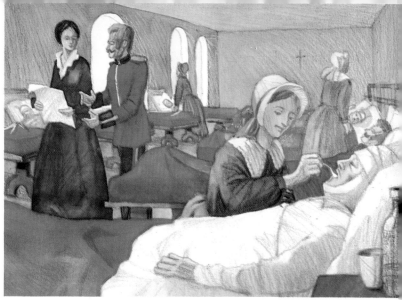

In Spain there was no running water in the large towns, and the rich took two baths a year! There were firms who supplied them with baths at home. They rented bathtubs and carried in the water.

Florence Nightingale trained as a nurse in Germany; there were no British nursing schools. She tended the wounded in the Crimean War, became a national heroine, and made nursing respectable.

The watering places of France and Germany were very popular, and members of European high society used to gather in the summer at spas like Baden Baden in Germany. Doctors recommended the spring waters for the health because they were rich in mineral salts.

Taking a sauna was a regular event in Scandinavia, and families used to take them together in special wooden cabins. Water was thrown onto white-hot stones to fill the cabins with steam. The hot steam bath was followed by a cold shower.

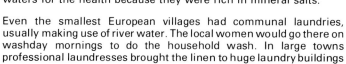

Even the smallest European villages had communal laundries, usually making use of river water. The local women would go there on washday mornings to do the household wash. In large towns professional laundresses brought the linen to huge laundry buildings

with enormous tubs. The linen was cleaned in steam rooms and then rinsed. Then the different items, all numbered, were handed out to women in different parts of the town who ironed them, perfumed them, and delivered them back to the middle-class homes.

The joys of sport and the delights of tourism

The English words *sport* and *tourism* were on the lips of everyone in Europe. It was the English—the richest and most cultured people in Europe—who traveled the most widely and who started to organize sports and team games. Of course, the English hadn't invented sports. All over Europe people with time and money were enjoying croquet, skating, archery, fencing, and sea and freshwater bathing. Horse racing was popular in both England and France. In Paris, people bowled on the Champs-Élysées, and an English nobleman, Lord Arsouille, taught *savate* (boxing with hands and feet) in the working-class districts. The Germans had shooting clubs, and the Spanish thronged to watch bullfights.

But it was the English who invented competitive sports. Cricket had long been popular; now football (soccer), once a rough country game, was revived on the playing fields of the great public schools. Rugby football was invented at Rugby School in 1823. Matches between school and university teams began drawing crowds of spectators.

The English were enthusiastic tourists, too. They swarmed over Europe and reveled in the newly popular sport of mountaineering. The shrewd Swiss built hotels on their mountain peaks. People climbed on foot, on horseback, or in chairs carried by porters.

In 1850, people often traveled for sentimental reasons. The English crossed the sea to visit Waterloo; the French went to Golfe Juan where Napoleon had disembarked on his return from Elba. Tourists went to Vaucluse in memory of Petrarch and to Ravenna in honor of Dante. Of course, these were expensive trips. But the package tour was soon to follow. In 1841 an Englishman, named Thomas Cook, arranged the first group railway travel, and by the 1860s he was organizing tours to Europe, the United States, and the Middle East.

Those who couldn't afford to go abroad could take a train to seaside resorts, like Brighton in England and Trouville on the Normandy coast, where the writer Alexandre Dumas had started a fashion for sea bathing by plunging into the waves stark naked! Sea bathing was usually much more proper. Men and women bathed separately. The ladies would enter the water from bathing machines, wooden cabins on wheels. They were well covered by their bathing costumes!

Rowing was a popular sport with the famous English public schools. Every year new teams were picked, and schools like Eton and Harrow raced each other on the Thames. The first boat race between Oxford and Cambridge, which is still held annually, was in 1829 at Henley, where the famous annual regatta started ten years later. In 1851 Prince Albert attended, and the event became known as the Henley Royal Regatta. There was a fashion for regattas in France, too, with many races held on the Seine.

Travelers in search of historical sites bought the famous guidebooks written by the German publisher Karl Baedeker. They contained all the information one could possibly need; for example, where to hire donkeys in Spain to ride in the Pyrenees.

In the park of the Palace of Tsarkoy Selo, the ladies of the Russian court were pushed around an ice rink in chairs fixed on sledges. This graceful sport took place at night, lit by torches; very often they swirled around to the music of a band.

Public swimming pools were being opened, like the Deligny baths in Paris. They were opened in 1842, on the Seine, whose water was very pure. Instructors taught the breaststroke, crawl, and diving.

In England prizefighting was frowned on. It could be very brutal and drew rowdy crowds who came to bet. But it was difficult for the law to interfere because matches were patronized by the aristocracy.

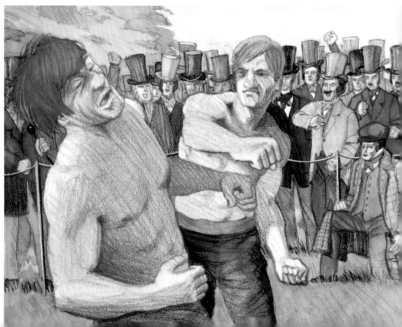

A hundred million children with no education

Education in Europe in 1850 was a disaster. There was no such thing as compulsory schooling. In France, a highly civilized country, there were over 3,000 communities with no schools. One child in three had no formal education. England was even worse off, with only half the number of schools as France. Russia had none at all.

The children of the poor were at work in fields, factories, mines, or shops—or simply roaming the streets. In England some went to the national or British schools, grim, overcrowded places organized by churches, where they learned just enough to read the Bible. For waifs and strays the earl of Shaftesbury started "Ragged Schools," which kept the children off the streets but taught them little.

Better-off European families employed tutors for their sons or sent them to board at various kinds of private schools—French *lycées,* German *gymnasia,* or English public schools. These famous English schools, like Eton, Harrow, and Rugby, were attended by the sons of the upper classes. They were much improved at this time, with a broader education, less bullying, and a stress on religion and organized games. Girls were usually taught at home by governesses, though there were some girls' schools. Everywhere discipline was harsh and the food was poor. Children were not expected to enjoy learning, and were often caned. In France they were marched into the classroom to the rhythmic beat of a drum.

The brightest pupils went on to a university. Oxford and Cambridge in England and some German universities, like Heidelberg and Gottingen, provided an excellent higher education for the sons of the rich. In France, only one in seven of those who had received a secondary education went on to study for a profession, most of them in Paris. The accent at universities was on literature, Latin, and Greek; however, the students of the day included scientists like Louis Pasteur and Charles Darwin.

At the famous University of Heidelberg, the students fought in duels in the German fashion, using cavalry sabers. They were not considered manly unless they finished their studies with scars on their faces. Students were patriotic, too: they wanted a unified German nation centered on Prussia. Professors who supported unification were popular with these students, but they were refused entry to other universities who were hostile to Prussia. Gottingen, which was famous for its library, was one of the hostile institutions.

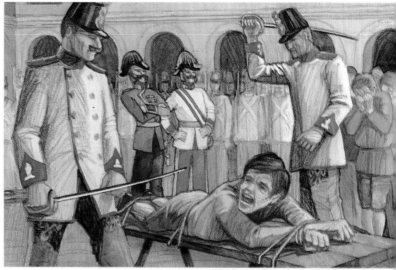

Not every child could go to school, for there simply were not enough schools. In the West Indies the colonial estate owners established boarding schools for the children of their workers. Students slept in hammocks, like sailors.

In England, orphans and the children of the very poor were placed in special charity schools called "Ragged Schools." The school mistresses taught there in return for their board and lodging, often receiving no other pay.

At Bratislava University in Czechoslovakia, the students demonstrated in support of independence for their country, which was under the rule of Austria. Soldiers were brought in to restore order. They arrested the students and beat them.

The English aristocracy sent their sons to Oxford or Cambridge university. During their three years there, they learned Greek and Latin. There was much stress on boxing, football, rowing, and the rather affected manners of the upper classes.

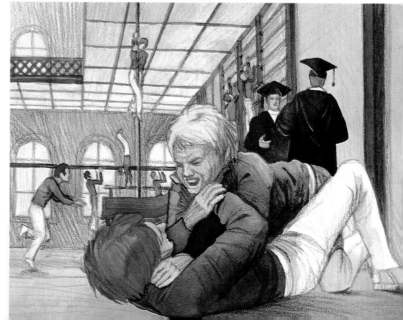

Street games and toys

On the streets, in farmyards, in village squares— there were children everywhere. Between 1800 and 1850 the population had doubled, and there were a lot of very young people about. They ran in groups in streets, parks, and public gardens. Those with parents at work had no one to look after them. Those without parents grew up in gangs. Free to follow their own devices, they lived as best they could by foraging and stealing.

Street children could play all day at knuckle-bones, leapfrog, "cops and robbers," marbles, and hopscotch. They could watch the free shows in the streets and public gardens—strolling musicians, jugglers, bear trainers, and organ-grinders with their monkeys. They would beg for a penny or two to ride the merry-go-round or visit a cheap theater. At Christmas, English children sang carols outside the houses of the rich, who would give them money or food.

In France, children who found an orange at the foot of the Christmas tree could count themselves lucky.

Only rich children had expensive toys—mechanical dolls, dolls' houses, and toy tea sets for the girls; lead soldiers and rocking horses for the boys. They had card games and toy theaters with cutout characters. Books were being written for children, too. But the children of the rich were brought up strictly, and didn't always have more fun than poor children.

Country children made their own toys. They carved wooden whistles and pipes. They made swords, guns, carts, wooden water mills, and crude dolls for the girls. And then there were local fairs with lots of amusements for children. Among the favorites were donkey rides and sack races.

But playtime didn't last long, and the merry childhood bands were soon scattered. At eight or nine, most children had to go to work. Only a few went to school.

In the parks of Rome, the children of the rich imitated their parents, riding about in pretty little carriages drawn by goats. The girls vied with each other in dressing elegantly and behaving like proper little ladies.

The Chinese Shadow Theater had been introduced to France in the 18th century by a showman called the Grand Séraphin. His son carried on the tradition in the arcades of the Palais Royal in Paris, drawing eager, round-eyed young audiences.

There were no "green spaces" in the working-class districts of the big towns. But there were public gardens where the more affluent children could play on Sundays. In Paris there were the Tuileries, the Champs-Élysées and the Tivoli gardens, which were always crowded

Toy manufacturing had made a lot of progress. There had been dolls that could walk and talk since 1823. Some of them could open and close their eyes. Poorer children had only simple dolls made of wood, papier mâché or rags.

with people taking the air. Children played there with hoops, shuttlecocks, and skipping ropes. There were strolling vendors who sold them oranges, barley sugar, spice cakes, and a drink called "coco," a mixture of licorice, water, and lemon juice.

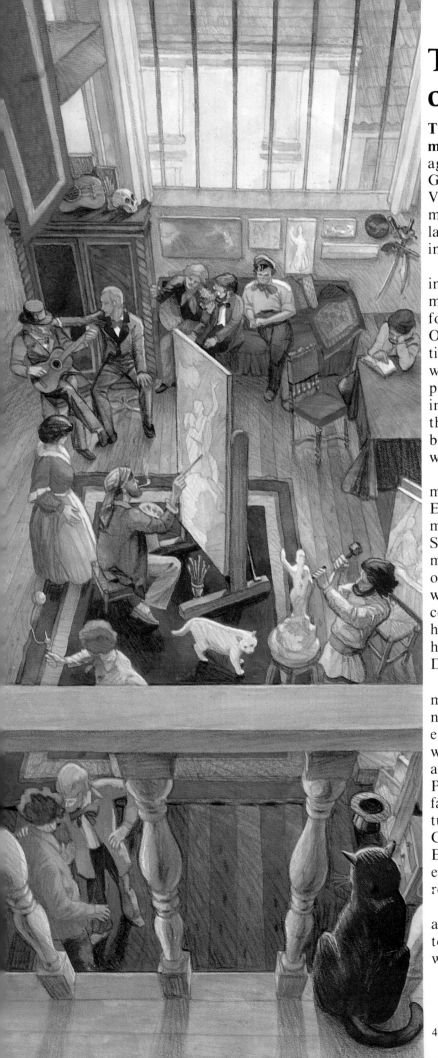

The champions of progress

The march of progress was bound to change both man and the world he lived in. All thinking men agreed on that, whether they were German like Georg Hegel, French like Joseph Renan, Italian like Verdi, or Russian like Tolstoy. Clearly, developments in chemistry, biology and physics—particularly electricity—were heralding a new leap forward in industry and technology. But what about man?

Thinking people were concerned about preventing humanity from becoming slaves to machines and money. In France, Saint-Simon had already put forward his socialist ideas. In England, Robert Owen, a cotton-mill owner, tried to organize production and protect the workers. Novelists, like Dickens, were writing about social injustice, and the philosopher John Stuart Mill was proclaiming the rights of individuals, including women, to free life and thought. In 1848 Karl Marx and Friedrich Engels, both Germans, published the *Communist Manifesto* with its message, "Workers of the world, unite!"

While some people were trying to improve man's life, others were fascinated by his past. Europeans traveled to Greece and Egypt, filling museums with the antiquities they brought back. Some people were busy restoring ancient monuments, like the architect Viollet-le-Duc who worked on Notre Dame Cathedral in Paris. In England there was a fashion for building in the "Gothic" style copied from the Middle Ages. Serious works of history were widely read, and people devoured historical romances by Walter Scott and Alexandre Dumas.

The wind of change was blowing away outmoded ideas. Artists, writers, and composers were no longer content to be romantic dreamers or mere entertainers. They wanted to produce works that would move the masses. Wagner's *Flying Dutchman* and Verdi's *Il Trovatore* revolutionized opera. Painters wanted to reproduce life as it was, with no false pretenses. In France, Honoré Daumier caricatured the faults of the middle classes, and Gustave Courbet painted the poor with moving realism. The English Pre-Raphaelite artists painted pictures of everyday life or chivalrous romance in minute, realistic detail.

Artists, writers, and thinkers formed the secret army of progress. They believed they had a mission to teach men how to achieve a better life through work and cooperation.

Novels were often written as newspaper or magazine serials. The authors would collect a weekly payment when they delivered the latest episode, eagerly awaited by the public. The French writer Honoré de Balzac, wrote his best novels that way.

The French socialist philosopher Claude Henri de Saint-Simon had died in 1825, but his disciples followed his principles. They lived in a community at Ménilmontant, just outside Paris. They all dressed the same and cooked and cleaned for themselves like monks.

The Great Exhibition of 1851, the first international exhibition, was opened by Queen Victoria and Prince Albert in London's Hyde Park. It was housed in a gigantic building called the Crystal Palace. It was built in metal and glass; no stone, cement, or brick was used; even the pillars were of iron. Six million visitors flocked to see examples of brand new industrial machines, as well as works of art from all over the world. Thomas Cook's railway excursions enabled working class folk from outside London to visit the exhibition.

The British were fascinated by archaeology. They crossed the Mediterranean to collect ancient masterpieces to put in the British Museum; these giant statues from Nineveh were brought by boat from Mesopotamia.

In Paris the Italian opera was all the rage. Some of the stage effects were very expensive to put on; for example, when the director wanted to reproduce ocean waves, he would hire a whole army of stagehands who had to move up and down under a vast sheet.

The birth of the popular press

The era of the cheap daily paper came into being, thanks to technology and the efforts of newspaper owners like John Walter, whose father had founded the London *Times* in 1785, and Emile de Girardin, who started *La Presse* in Paris in 1836.

News could travel fast now. Rotary printing presses and papermaking machines could produce papers quickly and cheaply. Stories could be sent rapidly by electric telegraph. Most important of all, the railways enabled papers to be delivered daily, even to country districts.

The early press lords had a lot to offer, above all the attraction of the news, which took first place in their columns. Everyone who could read wanted to be well informed, and the press became an open window on the world. Press agencies started, like Reuters and Havas. Travel stories were sent in by globe-trotters, the forerunners of today's roving reporters. From the Crimea, William Russell sent back powerfully written dispatches on the horrors of the war in that area.

By the 1850s there were about six morning papers in London, including the popular *Daily News* co-founded by Dickens in 1846. It was not much concerned with politics, but was packed with news items. Some papers, however, were founded for purely political purposes. In France, Italy, and Germany, they included papers like *Le Journal* that attacked authoritarian regimes. There were also socialist papers that were widely read.

The public also read for entertainment, devouring the weekly serials written by Dumas, Balzac, and Dickens, who also founded a weekly, *Household Words* (price 2 pence), one of many popular magazines. Advertising was becoming important, too. The English enjoyed reading the "small ads" advertising jobs and patent medicines. And when the *Illustrated London News* was launched in 1842, two hundred men paraded the streets of London carrying placards to announce the event.

42

Some western European papers already had very large circulations. English dailies were in the lead with the *Times,* read worldwide by about 59,000 people. In Paris and Cologne, too, papers were being produced cheaply. When Emile de Girardin sold *La Presse* for only 15 centimes, its sales increased rapidly. Editors commissioned famous writers to write serials. Many well-known books appeared in this way, like Dumas's *Three Musketeers,* many of Dickens's novels, and in America, Harriet Beecher Stowe's *Uncle Tom's Cabin.*

In 1851 the first electric telegraph cable was laid under the sea between England and France, and press agencies were now able to send out news instantly. Charles Havas of Normandy started his Paris agency, and the German Paul Reuter set up an office in London.

This machine, invented by the Italian Marinoni, was used to print the French newspaper *La Presse.* It produced 1,500 copies an hour for each of its cylinders. Machines like this meant that more and more paper could be printed at a more economical cost.

Newspaper sellers set up stands in the streets of Paris. The police kept an eye on them, for some of the newspapers they sold were subversive and were forbidden by law.

The expansion of the railways and postal services helped newspapers to reach a wider public. Traveling postal wagons, like this one, enabled the mail to be sorted during journeys.

Sunday outings

Everyone enjoyed Sundays and holidays. English countrymen played skittles, French peasants went poaching, Russian *mujiks* drank and danced. In the towns, people of all classes went out walking, on the Champs-Élysées in Paris, on the Ring in Vienna, on the Unter den Linden in Berlin. The boulevards of Paris and Barcelona teemed with workers who came in from the dreary suburbs to enjoy a few hours of city life. In Moscow, they could let off steam by tobogganing down enormous slides.

There were many more amusements than there are today. In Paris, there was the *Concert Musart* on the Champs-Élysées, the "Russian Mountains" in the Jardin de Paris, and a circus where 6,000 spectators could laugh at the brilliant clown Auriol. Opposite this was the "Castle of Hell" showing magic and conjuring shows.

English people were not supposed to enjoy themselves on Sundays! But there was plenty for them to do on holidays and in the evenings. London, like Paris, was full of theaters, marionette and puppet shows, and "panoramas" and "dioramas" showing huge pictures of famous views in a revolving room. There were pleasure gardens, too. Vauxhall was becoming rather rowdy, but in 1843 the Cremorne Gardens were opened, attracting cheerful Cockney crowds with a circus, theater, sideshows, fireworks, and open-air dancing.

Although only the wealthy could travel from the provinces to enjoy the delights of the city, there were plenty of circuses, theater troupes, and menageries traveling around the small towns and villages of Europe. Country people liked curiosities and enjoyed shows of freaks, like the "five-legged calf" or the "bearded lady." Their imaginations could take a holiday, too!

The "Georama" in Paris was as popular as planetariums are today. A map of the world was reproduced on the inside walls of a round chamber. Great numbers of people enjoyed visiting it.

In Belgium the September Festival, on the anniversary of national independence, was celebrated by huge fairs. One of the events was "Flemish jousting" in which dogcart drivers had to try to hit a target without spilling a bucket of water over themselves.

Open-air dance halls were popular in London and Paris. In Paris they were called "bals." One of the most famous was the Bal Mabille. It had been started by a dancing master called Mabille for his pupils. His sons expanded it into a huge park lit by 3,000 gas lamps. Famous

Young Parisians liked going to dance on Sundays at a place called "Robinson." In the giant chestnut trees, there were bowers where young lovers could be alone together. They were like little restaurant rooms, and were reached by a wooden stairway.

entertainers performed there, singers and dancers like "La Reine" Pomaré, Celeste Mogador, and Rigolboche, who danced the French cancan there for the first time in 1845. There were over 50 musicians. Entrance cost 5 francs for men and only 1 franc for women.

Governments and the governed

The king of Prussia and the czar of Russia had no parliament; the new emperor of Austria, Franz Joseph, didn't want one either. He had disbanded the one that his predecessor had agreed to form. Frederick William of Prussia, like his adviser Otto von Bismarck, detested "parliamentary chatterboxes."

The peoples of central and eastern Europe had to accept the decisions of their rulers and carry them out with as little argument as possible. Government ministers were backed up by huge and meddlesome administrations. In Russia and Austria they paid no attention to the protests of the people they governed. Very often these people—the Poles and Czechs, for instance—were not even Russian or German by nationality. But they had to obey like the rest, pay their taxes, and do military service. In the West there was more freedom. Sometimes, as in France, those in power had violent arguments with the opposition, but at least the opposition was allowed to exist. Democracy had taken a step forward, too, in the way people were represented by their governments.

In London there had been a Parliament for a long time. It had two chambers, the noisy House of Commons, which had the power to throw the government out of office if it didn't like its policies, and the House of Lords, which could accept or reject the decisions of the Commons. But not everyone had a right to elect members of parliament. In 1832, following country-wide riots, the vote was extended to the middle classes—"£10 householders"—but the workers who had taken part in the riots were still excluded.

In France the principle of "universal suffrage" was accepted in 1848 and was never again disputed. Every man over 21 had the right to vote. But they had to wait nearly thirty years before the Chamber of Deputies had any real power of control. All the same, the French got into the habit of voting. In the 1848 elections, villagers went on foot in happy bands to their county headquarters to place their votes in urns. Since most of them couldn't read, they would ask the local priest, the lord, or sometimes the village schoolmaster for advice.

Switzerland, Sweden, Belgium, and the Low Countries all had parliaments, but there were none as yet in Spain, Greece, or Italy, except for Piedmont in the north.

The Austrian court had a highly organized system of etiquette. Court life followed a succession of well-regulated ceremonies in which each move was fixed in advance. Every summer at the Castle of Schönbrunn the emperor Franz Joseph celebrated the Grand Royal

Festivities. The centenary of the founding of the Order of Maria Theresa was a particularly impressive event. There were fewer than 500 members in the Order; only especially deserving princes and noblemen were granted the honor of joining.

English peers, rich from birth and educated in the best schools, had an automatic right to enter the House of Lords. In the 1850s they had quite a lot of influence, and the chief ministers were usually lords.

In Russia there were no members of parliament. The czar sent out army messengers or the police to announce his decisions, which were read out in the village squares. He ruled with an iron rod.

The Austrians, who occupied much of Italy, threw anyone into prison who wanted to turn his country into a united and independent nation. Many patriots spent ten years or more in prison cells, dreaming of a great future for their country.

In Paris there had been a Chamber of Deputies since 1814. Its members decided to use urns in which to place the votes so that they could be counted more quickly and easily. The votes were registered by small steel tokens, painted white for "yes" and blue for "no".

Religious conflict and renewal

In Europe in 1850 people were still being persecuted for their faith. The Russian czar insisted that all his subjects belong to the Orthodox Church. Polish Catholics were ill-treated; so were the Moslems whom the czar had recently conquered in Turkestan, and above all, the Jews who were victimized and attacked. In fact the Jews were oppressed all through central and eastern Europe.

The Catholics of England and Ireland had an uncomfortable time, while in Austria Franz Joseph persecuted non-Catholics. In Rome the pope re-opened the ghetto, a quarter reserved for the Jews; they were not allowed to go outside it.

There were few people who didn't attend a church, chapel, or synagogue. The Catholics of France, Britain, and Germany looked to the new pope, Pius IX. They no longer wanted to answer to states and governments and declared that the pope was the true leader of the Christian world. They believed that he alone could inspire the revival of faith needed to combat the irreligion and indifference of industrialized society.

There was a renewal of faith among Protestants, too. In England in the 1850s, there was a flood of religious books and moral paintings, and preachers spoke out fiercely against unbelief. Their fervor served to inspire the Calvinists in France and Switzerland and the Lutherans in Germany and Scandinavia.

Liberals were an active force, too, like the Swiss theologian Alexandre Vinet who promoted the cause of tolerance. He believed all religions should be given equal rights, as they were in the United States. They should not be supported by handouts from governments, but by contributions from their members. They should not be subjected to state supervision, nor serve the interests of the state. Vinet, like many other liberals—Catholics, Protestants, and Jews—fought equally for freedom of conscience and freedom for the individual churches.

48

In "Holy Russia" the czar had absolute control over the church. The Russian Orthodox Church was Christian, but for centuries it had rejected the authority of the pope in Rome. The czar appointed the dignitaries and priests of his church, who were called "popes." These priests were supported by the people of the villages, who brought them weekly offerings of food and other gifts. The czar was worshipped as God's representative. When he won a victory, the priests gathered the people together to sing a hymn in his praise.

Since the start of the century, the Jews of northwest Europe had had the right to practice their religion freely. On Saturdays they went to their synagogues to attend the service conducted by the rabbi.

The Roman Catholic Church liked dramatic demonstrations of piety. On Christmas Day, it was the custom for the pope to stand on the steps of Saint Peter's to bless a baby born during the night.

On New Year's Day the pope would appear on the balcony of Saint Peter's to give out his blessing, *urbi et orbi,* to the city of Rome and the Christian world. Pope Pius IX was very fond of this custom.

Scandinavian Protestants worshipped with simplicity, rejecting all ceremony. They met together in family groups in the villages. One of the elders would stand on a chair to read passages from the Bible.

The birth of modern warfare

Industry had already changed the face of war. Ships built of wood and cavalry charges were giving way to iron steamers and steel cannons. Fire power was a force to be reckoned with.

The English and French experienced this at first hand in 1854 when they went to war against Russia in the Crimea. During the famous Charge of the Light Brigade at Balaclava, the magnificent lancers and hussars of the British army were decimated. At Sebastopol both French and British suffered enormous losses from the enemy's bronze cannons before they finally got the better of the Russians.

The Russian Army, though powerful, was far from being the most modern in Europe. The Prussians and Austrians, now rivals, had made fantastic progress both in the manufacture of armaments and the art of war. They used railway cars to get men, horses, and cannons to the battlefield with speed. From now on, making war would involve more organization and planning than in the past.

The French and English were not badly provided for. They had good military academies like Saint-Cyr in France and had confidence in the power of their artillery, which they were always improving. England needed soldiers primarily for her colonies; the Indian Army was one of the jewels of the British crown. The French Army retained the uniforms of the First Empire with its infantry in bright red and blue, its fur-hatted grenadiers, and its prancing cavalry.

England's superiority lay more than ever with her Royal Navy, which dominated all the oceans of the world. After the Crimean War the British fleet acquired more and more screw-driven steamers, which were now being armored with steel plates. Their new grooved cannons could fire a distance of 3,000 yards compared with the old smooth bronze ones which could not fire 1,000 yards. The British Navy was at its peak and was to remain the finest in the world.

Discipline on board the ships of the British Royal Navy was the toughest in the world. The English citizen was the best protected by the law, but the British sailor was the worst treated. The ship's captain had complete rights over his men. Anyone who stepped out of line would be flogged or clapped in irons. Mutineers were hanged and their bodies flung into the sea in sacks. Sailors might spend months at sea without setting foot on land, so they had to take plenty of provisions with them, including live animals.

The German industrialist Alfred Krupp, the "Cannon King," was already the largest arms manufacturer in the world. He made the first steel cannon in 1847. His foundries were at Essen in the Ruhr, a region that was going through a great spurt of industrial growth.

In France young men of twenty had to attend a recruitment board. There they drew lots, and those who drew "bad" numbers had to join the army. Those with "good" ones could go home. Anyone who drew a "bad" number was allowed to pay someone to replace him.

The officers' school of Saint-Cyr practiced its maneuvers at the Satory Camp near Versailles. On Sundays middle-class Parisians used to visit the camp. The army put on splendid reviews, which their visitors much enjoyed. They admired the brilliantly colored uniforms

of the cavalry, and they were also well aware that the army was there to defend public order should there be a revolution. The workers had less liking for the military, who had fired on them during the uprisings of 1830 and June 1848.

Revolutionaries in action

Like a trail of dynamite, in 1848 the capitals of Europe were lit, one after the other, by the fire of revolution. It started in Paris on February 22. The workers put up barricades in the streets; the monarchy fell. Revolution soon spread to Italy via Turin, Florence, Venice, and finally Rome. In March it hit Germany and central Europe. On March 13 insurrection broke out in Vienna, and eight days later the workers of Berlin were rioting in the streets. Revolution reached Munich, Frankfurt, Prague, and Budapest. The ancient empires shook. Only England remained peaceful; in April a demonstration demanding votes for the workers took place without disturbance.

The insurgents everywhere were workers, and sometimes peasants, students, and the middle classes. They wanted to overthrow the old oppressive order. They demanded liberty and the right to work. They wanted to live, above all to live in freedom.

An economic crisis and shortage of food and work had created millions of victims. "Work and wages!" demanded the revolutionaries of Paris, Berlin, and Turin. The banks had financed railways, ports, and factories—why shouldn't they help the workers?

In Vienna and Berlin the peasants fought for the abolition of serfdom. The Germans, Austrians, and Italians wanted a say in political matters. They demanded constitutions and parliaments. The middle classes had had enough of obeying governments run by princes. They wanted English-style parliaments that would vote on laws and finance.

Many Europeans lived under occupation by foreign armies, and wanted to live in freedom. The Slavs, Czechs, Italians, and Hungarians rebelled against Austrian rule. The Poles wanted to stop being treated as Prussians or Russians and to be allowed to live freely as Poles.

This "springtime of nations" had no immediate results. The great powers restored order all over Europe with heavy-handed severity. The king of Prussia and the Austrian emperor remained monarchs of all they surveyed. The pope, who had fled, returned to Rome. Thousands of Parisians were deported and Napoleon's nephew, Louis Napoleon, who was expected to uphold law and order, was made president of France. But everywhere people had had a taste of independence, Nothing would stop them now.

The Austrians were detested in northern Italy, which they had occupied for a long time. The people of Milan rose up in revolt against them, aided by the soldiers of King Charles Albert of Piedmont.

At Stuttgart a parliament was formed which called for a constitutional government and the unification of the German states. Like all the other German parliaments, it was swept away.

At Vienna on March 13, 1848, the middle and working classes put up barricades in protest against the absolute rule of the Hapsburgs. The hated Prime Minister Metternich fled in a laundry cart, and Emperor Ferdinand agreed to the formation of a constitutional government. A

parliament met in September and freed the peasants from serfdom. But General Schwarzenberg's army recaptured Vienna in October and the parliament was dissolved. The emperor abdicated and was replaced by his nephew Franz Joseph.

The uprising in France was brutally suppressed. In June 1848, General Cavaignac broke up the revolt of the Parisian workers. Twenty-five thousand were arrested, and 11,000 deported. For a long time the revolutionary movement had no leaders.

In some German states the peasants were still living as they had in the Middle Ages. They had to give feudal dues and free labor to their lords. In 1848 they rebelled. The military were called out against them, but they did achieve emancipation from serfdom.

News about animals

France, 1832
The death is announced of Baron Georges Cuvier, zoologist and paleontologist, founder of comparative anatomy. This great scholar used to say that he had discovered his taste for natural history while coloring animal pictures.

Germany, 1837
The biologist Karl Ernst von Baer has just proved, as a result of his experiments on female dogs, that all mammals are born from eggs, called "ova."

Algeria, 1843
Colonel Carbuccia has assembled a corps of 100 dromedaries at Maison-Carrée.

France, 1845
The giraffe sent to King Charles X by the pasha of Egypt, Mehemet Ali, has just died at the Museum of Paris. It will be stuffed and put on show at the Museum of Verdun or La Rochelle. Its "sister," who was sent at the same time to King George V of England, died immediately upon arrival in that country, but in 1830 she was replaced by a pair of giraffes.

France, 1848
Some large packs of wolves are ravaging Normandy.

Russia, 1850
The czar has issued an edict forbidding the profession of bear training.

Algeria, 1850
A Frenchman called Gérard Juges, known as "the Frank," is becoming famous for his prowess as a lion-killer.

France, 1850
M. Poiteven, an aeronaut, created great interest in Paris by ascending on horseback with a balloon. The emotion of the spectators was very great and one lady fainted. He remained in the air an hour, seated on his horse.

Austria, 1852
The birth is announced of the first giraffe to be born in captivity in a European zoo, at the emperor's menagerie at Schönbrünn. A stable was specially prepared for it with a constant temperature of 17°C, day and night.

Algeria, 1852
Some Frenchmen have started the first ostrich farm in North Africa. In 1830 the Marseilles Zoological Gardens attempted a similar venture, but the business, which was financed by a local banker, failed almost immediately.

Algeria, 1853
The commander of the Barrail, who is said in certain circles to be the next war minister, has assembled near Laghouat the largest caravan of dromedaries to be formed since the start of the French invasion. It consists of no fewer than 1,800 animals.

Norway, 1854
The varying hare (*Lepus timidus*), which comes from the Faroe Islands in the North Atlantic, has just been introduced to Norway.

Germany, 1856
Professor Fuhlrott of Elberfeld has dug up near Düsseldorf the remains of a skeleton belonging to a primitive man from the Ice Age. He has named it "Neanderthal Man" after the region where it was found.

Germany, 1856
Dr. Kaup has been studying some curious fish caught in the sea. They look like transparent lily-of-the-valley leaves, and Dr. Kaup gave them the name of *Leptocephalus*. However, he has just realized that they are in fact larvae. These "fish," placed in an aquarium, changed after a time into eels.

England, 1857

A fine specimen of the whale tribe was driven ashore by gales on the Norfolk coast. When he found himself upon the land, he roared loudly and struggled most lustily to regain the deep.

Switzerland, 1857

A new bear pit has been opened at Berne. Some new occupants will be brought to replace the ones that were stolen in 1799 by French soldiers commanded by General Brune.

India, 1857

One of the most serious revolts ever to occur in the British Empire has just broken out in India. We are told that it started for religious reasons: the Hindu and Moslem troops object to cow and pork fat being used to grease the cartridges of their rifles.

Spain, 1857

Huge forest fires are raging through the province of Castile. It is believed that they were started by shepherds wanting to find new pastures for their flocks, which can amount to several million sheep at certain times of the year. An inquiry is in progress.

Australia, 1859

The sailors of the English clipper ship H.M.S. *Lightning* have set 24 wild rabbits loose on the continent. The results of this experiment are awaited with interest.

England, 1860

Ivory imports from Africa this year total 550,000 tons.

Near Teneriffe, 1861

On November 30, the French corvette *Alecton* had to fight off a giant octopus. The French writer Jules Verne is considering using this event as an episode in his next novel, to be called *Twenty Thousand Leagues Under the Sea.*

Germany, 1861

A curious fossil has been discovered in a slate quarry at Langenaltheim, Bavaria. It consists of a prehistoric reptile with feathered wings. Named the *Archaeopterix*, it is believed to be a very early form of bird.

France, 1862

A splendid edition has just been published of Perrault's *Fairy Tales* with striking and beautiful illustrations by Gustave Doré. We reproduce here a picture of "Puss in Boots," a perfect example of the originality and talent of an artist reaching new heights in contemporary animal painting.

Gibraltar, 1863

The number of Barbary apes living on the Rock has seriously diminished. It is said that there are only three left. The English have decided to import some new specimens from Morocco. There is a legend to the effect that when there are no more apes on the Rock it will cease to belong to the British Crown.

Morocco, 1866

As a result of the famine caused by the recent plague of locusts, 20,000 Moroccans have died of starvation.

France, 1868

The phylloxera, a small insect originating from America, has appeared in the vineyards around Avignon. It appears to be a serious threat to the plants.

China, 1869

In the Szechwan Mountains, a French Jesuit priest, Père Armand David, has discovered a curious kind of black and white bear, known as the Giant Panda. In 1865 Père David also discovered in China a hitherto unknown species of deer, which has been called "Père David's Deer."

The Golden Age of
THE HORSE

The appearance of the railways had little effect on horse breeding in Europe. In France alone there were still 2,900,000 horses. A great number of working horses were used in agriculture, the army, and road transport, and new styles of horse riding were being developed.

Racing in England...

The fashion for horse racing started in England. It was popular in the 12th century and was later encouraged by the Stuart royal family. In the 18th century the great landowners began selective breeding by importing purebred Arabian stallions. This created a new breed, the English thoroughbred, which was to distinguish itself on race courses all over Europe. It is said that all English thoroughbreds today are descended from just three Arabian stallions. The breed was fully established by the mid-19th century and had already been used to improve or develop other breeds, like the trotters of the United States and France.

In 1762 there were already 76 racecourses in Great Britain, with the Jockey Club (founded in 1751) as the governing body. By 1842, 1,218 races were being run every year, including some new Classic races like the 2,000 Guineas (1809) and the 1,000 Guineas (1814). Steeplechasing was regularized as a sport in the 19th century, the most important event being the Grand National, first run at Aintree near Liverpool in 1839. The course was, and still is, an extremely tough one. The jockeys and their mounts have to cover a distance of 4 miles, 856 yards, including 30 very difficult jumps.

English thoroughbreds

The dandy out riding, by Daumier

... And in France

Racing was taken up more slowly in France. The first regular course was laid down in 1776, supervised by the count of Artois, the future Charles X. In 1833 the French Jockey Club was founded by the duke of Orleans and his English friend Lord Seymour. But its members were really interested in it as a social club, so a separate society was formed later that year to encourage improvements in horse breeding. By 1834 there were 18 courses in France, and during the second half of the century there was a tremendous vogue for racing. In 1865 a Paris shopkeeper, Pierre Oller, invented a system of betting called *pari mutuel* ("bet among ourselves") from which the totalizator system was developed.

No pity for Gladiator (a famous horse who had lost a race) Caricature by Bertall.

A member of the French Jockey Club and his groom Caricature by Stop.

The French school of equitation

Although the English were renowned for their fine horses and their racecourses, it was the French who took the art of riding seriously during this century. The Cavalry School of Saumur, reorganized in 1825 by Marshal Oudinot, produced three of the most brilliant horsemen ever known— the Viscount Aure, nicknamed "the Centaur," chief instructor at the school from 1847 to 1855; François Baucher, son of a wine merchant; and General Lhotte, who was given his first lessons by Baucher before studying under Aure, whom he succeeded. Baucher became famous by showing off his skills in a circus. One of his pupils, the English-born James Fillis, became chief groom at the court of the czar of Russia.

Birds and Animals

LE PERROQUET TAPIRÉ.

L'ARA VERT.

The bird seller. Caricature by Cham.

THE POPULAR PARROT

Many people were interested in natural history at this time, and a number of amateur naturalists began collecting birds, both stuffed and alive. Regular consignments of exotic birds arrived from the West Indies, South America, and Africa, and a favorite species was the parrot. Of course, sailors had been bringing back parrots from their travels since Roman times, but now people began to keep numbers of them in aviaries, as well as having them as pets. One very fine collection was owned by the Regent's Park Zoo in London, and in 1830 Edward Lear, then aged 18, was asked to make drawings of them. Lear is best known for his nonsense verses for children, but he was a serious artist too. His portfolio of 42 colored lithographs of the zoo's parrots was very well received. He then went on to illustrate the famous collection of birds owned by the earl of Derby at Knowsley Hall, now a safari park. Lear became very fond of the parrots while he was drawing them. He made a self-portrait showing one roosting on his head, and later on he decorated his books with little parrot drawings.

Another famous parrot illustrator was John Gould, who traveled as an artist with Charles Darwin on his famous voyage south on the *Beagle*. In 1838 he returned to Australia with his wife, and between 1840 and 1848, he published a huge work, *The Birds of Australia,* consisting of seven large volumes illustrated with 681 hand-colored plates. He also brought back the first budgerigars to Europe, which created quite a sensation. In 1884 the Australian government became anxious about the demand for their birds, and banned further exports. Most of the parrots in Europe today are descended from those imported between 1840 and 1884.

Parrots were extremely popular in France. In 1837 the writer Stendhal spoke of the street in Beaucaire in the Midi "where the parrots chatter about their voyages." In 1847 the countess of Armaillié described the port of Le Havre where "one's head swims with the cries of the sailors and those of the parrots whose cages clutter the narrow streets." Celebrated parrot owners included the duchess of Berry, whose aviaries were famous at court, and the poet Alfred de Vigny whose parrot, it was said, never wanted to leave his side. A fashionable German physician, Dr. Koreff, kept two talking parrots to amuse his lady patients, and Alexandre Dumas had a splendid aviary built at his Château of Monte Cristo. Marie Duplessis, the original "Lady of the Camellias" had a superb blue and yellow macaw which was sold after her death in 1847 for the huge sum of 230 francs.

The Paris bird market

in Fashion

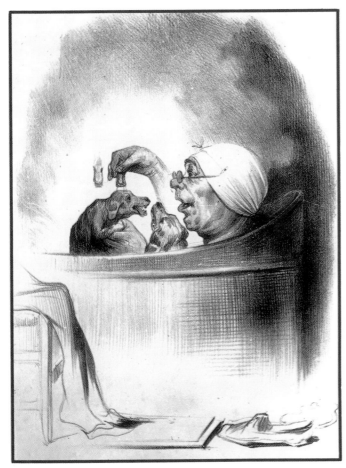

The family bath. Caricature by Daumier.

SOME UNUSUAL CATS AND DOGS

There was a growing fashion for keeping animals as pets, and several new breeds appeared. The first Abyssinian cat was brought to England in 1869, and the first pair of Siamese to be officially imported arrived in 1884. They were a gift from the king of Siam to a Mr. Owen Gould. The discovery of microbes, incidentally, made cats much more popular; since they were always washing themselves, they were thought to be very hygienic animals!

Dog shows began to be organized from 1859 onwards, and systematic attempts were made to maintain breeds and create new ones. These included the retriever (bred in 1807 from the Newfoundland); the miniature Yorkshire terrier, first seen at dog shows in 1861; and the Dandie Dinmont, which was immortalized in several paintings. Then there was the Brittany spaniel (there was a mania in Brittany for all things English), the Bedlington terrier (a favorite sporting dog of miners), and the short-haired fox terrier. This last was used for an unpleasant sport, ratting, which had been popular in England since the 16th century. A number of rats were hemmed into a pit by a wire cage, and a terrier was put in with them. Bets were laid as to which dog could kill the most rats in the shortest time. In the 19th century there were about 40 rat pits in London, and the sport was introduced to France, where it became all the rage.

Pointer

THE PREVENTION OF CRUELTY TO ANIMALS

As well as ratting, some other cruel sports were still popular, and animals like dray horses were often very badly treated by their owners. However, people were growing more concerned about animal welfare. In England the Royal Society for the Prevention of Cruelty to Animals had been founded in 1824. Bull and bear baiting were banned in 1835 and cockfighting in 1849 (though it still went on in secret). In 1850 the French parliament, despite some opposition, passed a law to protect animals, and in 1860 the French Society for the Protection of Animals was recognized as a public service by Napoleon III. A similar society was formed in Switzerland. Yet in Germany in 1860, a man called Karl Kreutzberg was trying to revive animal combats in the style of Ancient Rome.

Louis Pasteur
saves the silk industry

ALÈS, France, 1865.   A serious disease is threatening to ruin the silkworm industry in the Midi region, and 3,500 local silk farmers have called in the scientist Louis Pasteur, famous for his study of fermentation and his method of preserving beer, called "pasteurization."

Shortly after his arrival in June 1865, the celebrated biologist ascertained that the mysterious sickness, which is ravaging the nurseries, kills off the precious larvae before they have time to spin their cocoons. The local people, who have named the disease "*pébrine*," have been trying unsuccessfully to treat it with old wives' remedies. Unfortunately, before he had time to make further progress, Louis Pasteur was summoned by telegram to the side of his father, whose health was giving cause for concern.

1866.   Louis Pasteur has returned to Alès, sent by the Ministry of Agriculture. It is announced that he has found a method of eliminating the disease that attacks the silkworm eggs.

1869.   While resting for a few weeks at Saint Hippolyte-du-Fort, Pasteur has decided, with the help of some colleagues, to make a study of a new silkworm disease called "flaccidity." As a result of painstaking research, he has already isolated in the intestines of the sick larvae a streptococcus and a bacillus that could be causing the infection.

TRIESTE, Italy.   This year's silk harvest on the ancient Borghese estate has brought in 26,000 gold francs, the first profits for ten years. The silk farm has been saved by the work of Louis Pasteur; this followed his success with *pébrine* in France and Corsica.

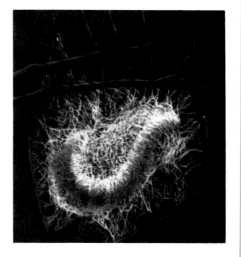

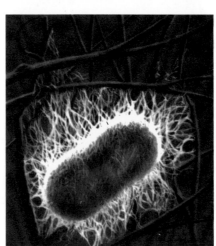

Louis Pasteur, born at Dole in the Jura in 1822, is best known for his discovery of the anti-rabies vaccine in 1886, and is credited with saving the French wine and silk industries. A chemist and biologist, he first showed that the process of fermentation was not, as was then believed, the result of "spontaneous generation," but was caused by the action of microorganisms. After studying silkworm diseases and developing a method of preserving beer and wine by "pasteurization," this indefatigable scientist threw his energies into the study of microbes between 1870 and 1886. He discovered the staphylococcus (the microbe responsible for septicemia) and developed a vaccine against anthrax, a very serious infectious disease that was killing hundreds of horses, cattle, and rabbits. In 1888, seven years before his death, the Pasteur Institute was founded to carry on his work in microbiology, the new field created by Pasteur.

A silkworm making its cocoon. With the aid of a framework of twigs, the larva secretes a fluid from glands near its mouth that hardens into a silk thread which it spins into a cocoon.

GLOSSARY

Agriculture Farming

Anesthetic A substance that causes loss of the feelings of pain, touch, or cold

Archaeology The study of the people, customs, and life of ancient times

Aristocracy Any class that is considered superior because of birth, culture, or wealth

Armaments War supplies and equipment

Artisan A workman who is skilled in some industry or trade

Boyard A member of the high-ranking Russian aristocracy

Cholera An infectious disease of the stomach and intestines

Clipper ship A sailing ship built and rigged for speed

Democracy A government that is run by the people

Diphtheria An infectious disease of the throat

Emigrate To move out of one's own country and settle in another

Epidemic The rapid spreading of a disease so that a large number of people have it at the same time

Factory A building where products are manufactured

Famine A lack of food in a place; a time of starvation

Fertilizer An organic or chemical substance put on land to help it produce more and better crops

Foundry A place where metal is melted and molded

Guild A union of workers in one trade or craft

Industrial Revolution The change to an industrial society from an agricultural one, and to factory production from home manufacturing

Mujik A Russian peasant

Omnibus A large vehicle with seats inside and also on the roof

Opera A play that is mostly sung

Parliament The highest lawmaking body of a country

Pasteurization The process of heating (milk, beer, or wine) to a high temperature and then chilling it to kill off harmful bacteria

Pauper A person who is supported by charity

Peasant A farmer of the working class

Peer A man who has a title such as duke, earl, count, or baron

Philospher A person who studies the truth and principles behind all knowledge

Poaching Trespassing, hunting, or fishing on someone else's land

Poverty The state of lacking money

Public school A private boarding school in England

Reaper A machine that cuts grain or gathers a crop

Revolution A complete overthrow of an established government

Serf A slave who belonged to the land he worked on and was bought and sold along with the land

Shepherd A person who takes care of sheep

Skittles A game like bowling in which one tries to knock over nine wooden pins by rolling balls or throwing wooden disks at them

Socialism A system of social organization in which the government controls the means of production and distribution of goods

Steamship A ship powered by steam

Strike A work stoppage to enforce demands for better wages, shorter hours, or improved benefits

Suburb A community just outside of a city or large town

Suffrage The right or privilege of voting

Telegraph An electrical system for sending messages

Textile A woven fabric

Trade union An association of workers in the same trade or craft whose purpose it is to protect and promote their interests

University An institution of higher education

Wages An amount paid for work

Watering place A resort where people enjoy bathing, boating, sports, etc.

Workhouse A place where very poor people are lodged and given work

INDEX

1 2 3 4 5 6 7 8 U 88 87 86 85 84 83

OVERSIZE